THE FUNNIEST HAUNTED HOUSE BOOK EVER!

What is worse than
seeing a ghost?
Seeing two ghosts.

By Joseph Rosenbloom
Illustrated by Hans Wilhelm

 Sterling Publishing Co., Inc.   New York

What do you hear when you
knock on the door of a
haunted house?
  "WHOOOOOOO's there?"

What goes around
a haunted house
but doesn't move?
  The fence.

Library of Congress Cataloging-in-Publication Data

Rosenbloom, Joseph.
  The funniest haunted house book ever! / by Joseph Rosenbloom;
illustrated by Hans Wilhelm.
      p.   cm.
  Summary: An illustrated collection of jokes and riddles about
ghosts, witches, monsters, and haunted houses.
  ISBN 0-8069-6818-4.—ISBN 0-8069-6819-2 (lib. bdg.)
  1. Riddles, Juvenile.   2. Monsters—Juvenile humor.
3. Supernatural—Juvenile humor.   4. Wit and humor, Juvenile.
[1. Jokes.   2. Riddles.   3. Horror—Wit and humor.]   I. Wilhelm,
Hans, ill.   II. Title.
PN6371.5.R6114   1989
818'.5402—dc19
                              88-38605
                                CIP
                                AC

Text copyright © 1989 by Joseph Rosenbloom
Illustrations copyright © 1989 by Hans Wilhelm, Inc.
Published by Sterling Publishing Co., Inc.
Two Park Avenue, New York, N.Y. 10016
Distributed in Canada by Oak Tree Press Ltd.
% Canadian Manda Group, P.O. Box 920, Station U
Toronto, Ontario, Canada M8Z 5P9
Distributed in Great Britain and Europe by Cassell PLC
Artillery House, Artillery Row, London SW1P 1RT, England
Distributed in Australia by Capricorn Ltd.
P.O. Box 665, Lane Cove, NSW 2066
Manufactured in the United States of America

Which monster can jump higher than a haunted house? *Any monster. A haunted house can't jump.*

Is it true that a monster won't touch you if you carry a flashlight? *That depends on how fast you carry it.*

How many vampires does it take to put in a light bulb?
None. Vampires like the dark.

Why did the vampire hit the clock?
Because the clock struck first.

Why do spiders spin webs?
Because they don't know how to knit.

What time is it when five monsters chase two ghosts?
Five after two.

How does a witch tell time?
With a witch watch.

What does a mother ghost
say to a little ghost who
talks too much?
"Don't spook until you're
spooken to."

How does a monster count to 32?
It takes its shoes off.

Where do lady monsters keep their hands?
In a handbag.

What part of a house makes a mummy nervous?
The living room.

Do mummies ever get presents?
Yes, on Mummy's Day.

What is white outside, green inside and hops?
A frog sandwich.

Why did the monster put three ducks in a carton?
He wanted a box of quackers.

What do little ghosts chew?
BOO-ble gum.

Why can't you join a monster in a glass of milk?
Because there isn't room for both of you in one glass.

What does a monster musician eat for breakfast?
Rock 'n' roll.

What did the monster do in the kitchen?
It beat the eggs, whipped the cream and battered the fish.

What part of a house does a
mummy like best?
The DIE-ning room.

What time is it when a
monster sits in a chair?
Time to get a new chair.

What scary creature do you find in a lunch box?
A sandwich (sand witch).

Which monster eats fried chicken with its fingers?
They all do. No monster takes off its fingers to eat fried chicken.

What is a ghost's favorite lunch?
Spook-ghetti.

What happens when the sandwich sees a ghost?
It becomes a scream cheese and yell-y sandwich.

Why don't mummies play
Hide-and-Seek?
They are all tied up.

Why don't monsters
play Hide-and-Seek?
*Who'd look for
them?*

What game do baby
ghosts play?
Peek-a-BOO!

How do mummies relax?
They unwind.

Why was the werewolf invited to the party?
Because he was a howl.

Why wasn't the zombie invited?
Because he couldn't be the life of the party.

Why wasn't the vampire invited?
Because he was a pain in the neck.

Why was the ghost invited to the party?
Because he was a scream.

What do you say when you meet a two-headed monster?
"Hello, hello!"

What do giants like to play at parties?
Swallow the Leader.

Why didn't the skeleton go to the party?
Because he had no-body to go with.

What happened when the werewolf fell into the washing machine?

He became a wash-and-wear wolf.

How do you know there is a giant in your dryer?

The door is hard to close.

GARY GHOST: You look dizzy. What happened?

LARRY GHOST: My mother put my sheets in the washing machine. She forgot I was still in them.

What steps should you take when a ghost chases you around a haunted house?
Giant steps.

What kind of ant is 15 feet tall?
A gi-ANT.

What do you do with a blue ghost?
Cheer him up.

What's pink and yellow
and goes "Crunch, crunch?"
*A monster eating crackers
in bed.*

What story do little
ghosts like to hear?
Little BOO-Creep.

In what room do you find
the most zombies?
The dead-room.

How do little ghosts play Indians?
With a BOO and arrow.

What comes out at night, wears a black cape and bites people? *A mosquito in a black cape.*

What is white, scares people and jumps 10 times a minute? *A ghost with hiccups.*

What story do little ghouls like to hear before they go to bed? *Ghouldilocks and the Three Scares.*

Why did the monster wear red suspenders?
To keep his shoulders down.

What is the difference between a furry monster and a flea?
A furry monster can have fleas, but a flea can't have furry monsters.

What do baby ghosts wear on their feet?
BOO-ties.

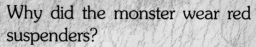

What do ghosts wear on their feet when it rains?
BOO-ts.

What do ghouls wear on their feet when it rains?
Ghoul-oshes.

What kind of fur do you get from a werewolf?
As fur as you can get.

Why did the werewolf wear a green belt?
To keep his pants up.

Why do werewolves wear fur coats?
Because they would look silly in plastic ones.

Why do werewolves wear big heels?
To keep their knuckles from dragging on the ground.

How do you keep a werewolf from ripping out the front seat of a car?
Make him sit in back.

What is the first thing a ghost does when he gets into a car?
He BOO-ckles his seat belt.

How do witches get
around fast?
*They fly their
bar-OOOOM sticks.*

What did the witch say
to the little broom?
"Go to sweep, wittle baby."

Why do witches fly
broomsticks?
*Because they don't
have tricycles.*

Why do witches have to
fly brooms?
*Because vacuum
cleaners don't have
long enough cords.*

What is the best safety
rule for witches?
*"Don't fly off the
handle."*

What do baby ghosts say
when they have to go
home?
   "BOO-hoo!"

What do two-headed
monsters say when they
have to go home?
   "Bye-bye!"

What does a hundred-foot monster say
when it has to go home?
   "So long!"